# The book of Irwin Gould
## (IDG) 2

The Book of Irwin Gould (IDG) 2: Bubbles and Sudz, plus
Copyright © 2024 by Irwin Gould

Published in the United States of America

Library of Congress Control Number: 2024923967
ISBN   Paperback:     979-8-89091-740-9
ISBN   Hardback:      979-8-89091-741-6
ISBN   eBook:         979-8-89091-742-3

All rights reserved. No part of this publication may be reproduced, stored in a retrieval system or transmitted in any way by any means, electronic, mechanical, photocopy, recording or otherwise without the prior permission of the author except as provided by USA copyright law.

The opinions expressed by the author are not necessarily those of ReadersMagnet, LLC.

ReadersMagnet, LLC
10620 Treena Street, Suite 230
San Diego, California, 92131 USA
1.619. 354. 2643 | www.readersmagnet.com

Book design copyright © 2024 by ReadersMagnet, LLC. All rights reserved.

Cover design by Ericka Obando
Interior design by Don De Guzman

# The book of Irwin Gould (IDG) 2

## Bubbles and Sudz, Plus

Irwin Gould

I started my business, **Bubbles and Sudz Plus**, a long time ago, back in 1998. In that time, I met some unique customers, many of whom set into motion miraculous interventions that defied all natural law and guided me to significant life lessons. I was so lucky as to have some of those customers guide me through the small and beautiful miracles that move me through this thing called everyday life. Believing in what I knew to be guidance from God, through His various signs, I began the trek down an unknown road toward an uncertain place that eventually became very certain! With faith and the joyful appearance of a few particular miracles, along with the everyday heavenly signals, the road became smoother and straighter and my Ray Bans certainly became less smudged. On I went, knowing that each step would lead to the next, and then to the next, while believing with faith in the fulfillment of the Greater Plan, the Plan that rewarded good and solid work as well as an understanding of how the puzzle worked. It just had to be figured out: where was it that I fit in the puzzle of life? Or, where we all fit in.

I moved to Florida from New York to work in the medical field along with a friend who happened to be my modeling agent. The medical facility company stored medical files for a south Florida hospital. I liked the job and thought it was great even though I was on call 24 hours. I was a supervisor and therefore had great responsibilities. During the first year working there, I had 12 employees working under me in the early morning shift. The work was good and I made decent money, but, I knew it was not enough to reach a satisfactory destination. I decided to walk ahead with a firm step and have a voice in my destiny. I, IDG, would start my own company. I had a vision of what it could be, something that was needed by everyone and something that would serve… a cleaning service! I needed more capital to just get moving. So, in addition to my full-time job, I took on a part time job working into the early evening. I operated a fork lift loading and unloading 18 Wheelers. Feeling it was still not enough, I took on yet another the part time job, working into the late evening, stocking shelves. It was quite the experience working 15 to 16 hours per day. And oh! I put in the work! So much so, I was able to save $11,000 in four months. It took hard work to accomplish this goal. It required self-discipline and the elimination of unnecessary spending on clothes and dining out, just to name a few. But, now the real journey began moving with earnest in fulfilment of this Great Plan which was still a bit of a mystery to me.

I needed a van, supplies, equipment and the wrap that advertised my services on the exterior of the van. In a short period of time, I learned a lot.

The starting point was evident: a van was the first item that had to be gotten. I did the research, went to several business locations and made a choice; I paid in cash. I took the van and got several estimates to wrap it for effective advertising and marketing of this new company, soon to be known as **Bubbles and Sudz Plus**. This was a very important step and more decisions had to be made. Whatever was wrapped on the van had to be professional with a winning design that would attract customers and win them over. The entire wrapping process would take 24 hours.

In that 24 hours, I moved on to the second task, and that was equipping the van to the greatest extent. The cleaning business was subject to a multitude of tasks so preparedness was essential. I ordered a 350-gallon water tank; a generator; a pressure washer; a vacuum. The business would also require brushes; tools; wax; cleaning supplies. Finally, a pegboard had to be gotten to set up the van in an orderly and efficient manner.

Once acquired, I opened the boxes of all the equipment and supplies and began setting up. The night progressed and in a couple of hours I was able to position everything as it would be laid out in the van.

The next morning, I received the call that the van would be done by late afternoon. I contacted the insurance company and legally, I was ready to go.

When I finally saw the van, I was amazed by the detail and the professional attention to quality. It was definitely a captivating design meant to draw in customers. I paid the remaining balance, got the keys and went home where I was able to finish the installation of all the equipment by early afternoon.

The next morning, I went to work at my fulltime job. I drove the new, beautifully wrapped van. By the time I got on Main Street, not more than two miles from home, I got my first call. There was a person driving behind the van and took the number from the back door. She inquired about a car detail and the price, and whether I could do it today in the afternoon. I said, "yes." I went to the gas station, got some gas for the equipment and texted her that I was on my way. Once I got to the house, I set up my equipment including the 4 cones out for safety for caution. I t was a four-door sedan car that needed good professional detail. I got to work. I filled up the bucket to wash the exterior of the car; I detailed the inside of the car, and steam cleaned the cup holders, the dashboard and the center console. I wanted to provide a great job. It was my first customer and I had to make a good impression. She came out and paid and then went to her car. It was so clean, she blew her horn and called me over to the car. She tipped

me again, turned and said that the car had never been so clean. I mentioned that I specialize in steam cleaning and that it's like night and day compared to traditional car detailing and that no other service specializes in steam cleaning. I was satisfied that I did a great job. I had no more calls for the day. I was finished working for the day. When I got home, I took a shower and prayed to God before I went to bed that evening: "Thank you, God, for giving me my first call and my first customer."

I kept my full-time job, and on the weekends, I detailed cars, pressure cleaned anything that needed it, and gave out business cards. Also, after 8 hours of work at the fulltime job, I detailed cars. Slowly, I built up my clientele. Everything went great but slowly; I continued to build up my customer base and made the extra cash, which I diligently saved. I learned that it takes a long time to develop full days of client appointments. Actually, it takes a few years. So, I kept my full-time job while continuing to grow my customer base on the side, believing that "this cog" would fit in the wheel somewhere.

For certain, one of the most interesting and impactful customers I encountered was 88 years old when I first met him. By that time, he had systematically built up a one–billion-dollar real estate empire. He was a humble man who found himself at the cusp of the evolution of the capitalist movement. He stepped into that, and while many failed, he

miraculously, succeeded. I loved his humility and his personal lessons. He believed that faithfully moving forward would lead to wonderful success. In his case, it did just that. Somehow, I felt a connection to this man. Was he in my Plan somewhere?

Time moved onward and his son wanted to be involved, going to work and dealing with the apartment complexes. My customer instructed his son that simply working with the complexes did not properly serve him or anyone because that was the easy part. He wanted his son to learn the law and the accounting process in order to preserve the equity. The son complied and eventually established his own law practice.

The time eventually arrived when my customer was 100 years old. In light of his father's age, my customer's son left his law practice and took over the family real estate business. Yet, his influence was ever-present; I knew it and I felt it. It was nourishing and fulfilling.

My respect for this man is great. At the time of his death, he was 100 years old and had been married for 72 years. His capital worth was $1.5 billion. His entire life was a platform for success. I greatly admired his work and vision; I knew that I could learn from him, mimic his Plan and move forward towards my own destiny.

The wonder of any miracle is enshrined in the unexpectedness of it. Its existence is heavily impressed on the mind and heart. And this is the manner in which I encountered my first miracle on a morning after I had just completed a job. I packed up the tools, got my payment and walked back to the van. For some unknown reason, I gravitated towards the passenger side door, opened it, and there, in that seat was a magnificent image of Jesus Christ. I couldn't believe my own eyes; I held my breath and my gaze for four seconds fearing that I would lose Him. But, I finally had to blink and after that the image was gone. I was awestruck. I knew God's presence surrounded me all the time, but never in my life did I ever imagine that I would be chosen as one to have such a heavenly experience. I remained silent on this; I slept on it for several days; I prayed for guidance. And on the fourth day, the Lord revealed Himself to me. He had given me a true miracle; He had given me an angel. But why? Was it to reinforce my faith in the glory of life? In the glory of another man's life?

Things moved on normally. I completed the detailing job of an RV and was satisfied with my work particularly on the exterior of the vehicle including the undercarriage and the top surface. The workweek was great and so was the weekend. I took advantage of wonderful weather with a focus on the word "wonder." How could I not "wonder" when meditating and praying while facing East towards the sunrise. After all, the Biblical Wise men saw the **star** in the East

and followed it to witness the birth of the King. Light comes from the East each and every day assuring me and millions of others that the Son of Man will return as sure as the sun rises. I follow it daily.

Monday morning arrived, as did the sun. What a way to celebrate the day but with the simple treat of coffee and orange juice from McDonalds. As I drove north towards Boca Raton, my eyes caught something unusual in the sky. There was lots of movement with twisting and turning and flashes of brown and white. Suddenly, I recognized that the scene of turmoil was actually a hawk carrying and struggling with prey in its beak. I brought the van to a stop at the red light but I couldn't stop watching the hawk in the battle of nature versus nature. Within seconds, the hawk lost grip on its victim which dropped, flailing, through air. The hawk tried to retrieve his prey but without success; yet, out of nowhere, another hawk swooped downward, caught the falling quarry and majestically flew away as the victor. I marveled at the scene. It was certainly unusual to witness such a performance in nature.

It was a sign; I was sure of it. Although I am not a fan of violence, having witnessed such, I acknowledged it as an affirmation of the Divine Order of the Universe in which I firmly believe.

In honor of that, I placed a print of the #12 above the passenger side door of the van, near where my angel appeared. The number 12 has significance;

it is mentioned in the Bible many times. There were 12 apostles; Jacob had 12 sons; there were 12 Tribes of Israel. The number has a presence in many other spots in the Bible and all are symbolic of God's great plan. I also placed 12 feathers in the visor of the van as a reminder of the hawks that I had seen. One of those feathers was found near my now-deceased elderly customer's home. For certain, the old man was still with me. I wondered what else he had to say to me.

The week moved on and work awaited. I arose early, faced the sun, said a prayer and headed out for my coffee and orange juice. I love my routines and order because they contributed to my strong and organized work habits. On this morning, I also had to stop for gas. After pumping the gas, I entered the 7-Eleven store and headed to the rear of the store where I picked up a couple of items. The only people in the store were the cashier and me. I put the items on the counter and returned to the rear to get a bag of ice. Not wanting to get the counter wet, I put the bag of ice on the floor next to my feet. In doing that, I saw money on the floor. I paid for the gas, the items and the ice. Then, I picked the money up; it was one hundred dollars! Was this a miracle? Had I gotten a sign indicating the beauty of the day to come?

I went to work; I did terrific work and enjoyed each minute of it. Indeed, it was a blessed day.

The following week was very hot and the schedule was filled. As usual, I stopped at Mickey D's for some breakfast. The job was rather large, a warehouse with lots of trucks, next to the salty ocean. I needed extra gas for this large job so at 5:00 AM, I stopped at 7Eleven to fill up. I entered the store, picked up some Gatorade and water and placed it on the counter. I went to the back of the store and got some ice and walked forward to the counter. Again, I placed the ice near my feet, and lo and behold, there, next to my feet and the ice, was cash! So weird! $60.00! I picked it up. I paid for my store items and the rest of the money was used for gasoline. Wow! How did this occur…again!

A referral came in. I needed to clean a car. The customer was a CPA and I had to go to his office to do the job. It turned out that he needed his car cleaned and he needed his hurricane shutters put on the office windows. He was an amenable fellow and spoke freely. He had been in practice for over 60 years and had a family which included a wife and two sons. In his musings, the man divulged some regrets regarding his family, sadly disclosing to his chagrin, the lack of ambition in his sons who experienced no success. They were lazy and spoiled and felt entitled and he realized his contributions to their state. One son was in jail and the other was a drug addict. All parents look forward to their children's greater success. He was clearly sad, which was so sad to me.

We finished up for the day, he paid me for the service and I thanked him sincerely. I left.

First thing the next morning, the CPA texted me, requesting that I come to his home in Aventura to put up that set of hurricane shutters. He reiterated that his sons were of no help to him or his wife. I performed various tasks for this man over a period of six months and each time we had a sincere conversation discussing many different topics, both serious and fun. I always looked forward to seeing him.

Of a sudden on a Monday morning, the CPA called to tell me that his son had passed away from a drug overdose in some unknown condominium. His voice was empty; I gently and sincerely offered my condolences. But, he continued telling me that he was going to change his will. In the event of both his and his wife's passing, over a half million dollars would be willed to the Salvation Army. I listened and wished him the best on his decision.

During those six months, I got to know the man rather well. He was in his late 70's or early 80's. He still worked seven days a week getting up between 4 AM and 5AM. Every time I was called to his home or business to pressure clean, he came outside to converse about everyday things. It felt as though we were friends and I truly enjoyed his company.

Things changed when his secretary of one year called to let me know that my friend the CPA had passed away. I couldn't believe it. And then, twelve months later, I was told his wife had passed away. Per the CPA's plan, his estate was donated to the Salvation Army.

In my mind, my friend the CPA, had fulfilled his final plan. But then, at another future moment, I would be called to stand fast for this man, pulling me straight into the light of truth and righteousness.

Life marched on and I moved each and every day knowing that I was part of God's Plan. That gave me great pleasure and peace. Facing east, I smiled at the sunrise welcoming each day. On a particular day, I headed out to a referred customer. As usual, I headed to McDonalds for a coffee and an OJ. Next stop was 7-Eleven for gasoline and daily supplies. I parked next to Pump #1 ready to pump gas for the van and the tanks. Down on the ground, at my feet, as though in gift, was money…again! This time it was $11.00. This time was different, though. I found the money outside and not in the confines of a store. I couldn't imagine where this was going. Hmmm…. message? I went inside and picked up a bag of ice and some Gatorade and paid for both items with the found money. I then put $100.00 on my credit card to put gas into the van and the containers.

This next customer was also a referral. I arrived at the location in Boca Raton near the beach. It was obvious that a very expensive neighborhood. I knocked on the door and I was welcomed in; we walked through the home to the patio area that was to be pressure cleaned. Lo and behold, the patio was directly next to the ocean, and moored there was a tremendous yacht. The customer points to the yacht and says that it is a $1 million vessel. I told him, "No man, I have never seen anything such as this yacht so close to a man's home." I gave him the estimate for his job and during that, in our conversation, he told me his history and work. He had been in business for over 40 years. I responded that since he had put in the years of work, he deserved everything that I was seeing.

I returned the next day to do the service still marveling at the sight of the yacht. I did a great job and was really satisfied with that. I continued to observe the fruits of good work and wondered where my path would lead. I believed that good people were rewarded and this was seen by me through the people I had met.

My belief in this was soon to be tested. The son of the CPA, the man who had changed his will because of the unreliability of his sons, called me for a favor.

The son knew that his father had developed a liking for me and that his father conversed openly

about both his sons. The son, who was recently released from jail, was interested in reclaiming the funds that his father had bequeathed to the Salvation Army. This son was asking me to testify that his father and mother were not of sound mind when they changed their will, that they were suffering from some sort of dementia, and that the change in the will was not representative of their true wishes.

My experience with the CPA was not in keeping with the son's apparent opinion. I experienced a completely coherent man and wife who understood both sons, each of whom never lived up to parental expectations, each of whom blatantly refused to become responsible adults and thus lost the overall trust of both parents. The parents never expressed anger, but rather acceptance of the situation.

Now, I was being asked to betray the CPA and his wife, and our sincere conversations to suit a son who betrayed his working parents. The father was clear in knowing both his sons, one who was a drug addict and the other who went to jail for robbery. He believed he offered proper loving guidance to both and both were disinterested in the business that took years to build. The CPA and his wife decided to will their money to a deserving entity, knowing that the surviving son would never be able to sustain and keep the business afloat because he never chose to attend college to pick up the necessary accounting skills. It was a sad decision, but, none-the-less, a decision. Who

was I to second-guess a man of his wits? A man who spoke in earnest to me? With this knowledge, I refused to cooperate with the errant son. I have no idea of the result of his endeavor. But I knew I was walking in the Light when I delivered this message to him.

While travelling to a referral customer, I had to stop at the United State Post Office to mail a package. I needed packing materials so I went over to that side of the lobby. In the process of choosing what I needed, I haphazardly looked down. Again, there was money on the floor! How could I not regard this as another miracle in my life? I picked up the money, found proper packing materials, and sent off the package using the $12 I had found. Was this another sign about the new customer?

I knocked on the door of the referral customer and introduced myself. The new customers were retired police officers who had served for 38 years. Combined, the couple had served almost 100 years in protecting American citizens. Throughout the year, I got to know these people. They told me much about their experiences in law enforcement. I found out that each of them had never had to draw a weapon; nor had either of them had a weapon drawn on them. I was astounded.

These people were my customers for a few years. One morning, the wife told me that her father was a police officer in Holland during World War II;

he too had never had to draw his weapon. When he came to the United States, he became a police officer and never once had he had to draw his weapon!

I began to see a pattern. When I find money, something special and unique is about to happen. That unique thing seemed to be related to the people I met through my business. The puzzle began to take form. To what was I to pay attention?

On another morning, I was again at a stop light. I am an observant individual and am constantly scanning the area. I couldn't help but notice a poor fellow crossing the street with two dogs in tow. One of the dogs had his tail up and seemed very happy, while the other dog was the opposite. He seemed forlorn, but accepting his destiny, as all three approached a trash can. The happy dog sat looking at his owner as the owner searched the trash bin for some scraps. The owner took the scraps out of the trash; the happy dog was so grateful that his tail kept wagging. The other dog conveyed his opinion of the scraps: his tail was down and his sad face looked away conveying, "I can't believe it; again, we are eating out of the rash can." He was definitely a sad little dog.

That workday ended; again, I was at the stop light. I couldn't help but notice the same man, with his dogs. Nearby was a lady at the bus stop who was waiting for the bus home. As she waited, she ate some food. The happy dog sat near the woman, wagging his tail and

listening to the conversation between the poor man and this woman. The second dog simply looked away knowing what his dinner would be on that evening, as well what was on the menu in the morning.

A wise man once said: When someone asks if you have eaten today, the reply is always, "Are you inviting? I am ready for another meal."

I make it my business to offer help and aid to such people whenever I can. The signs were apparent and I followed the message.

Life is like a gym; there will always be someone in better shape than you. But the ethic is that you are in competition with yourself. It is not about who is ahead or who is behind. It is about one's own progress or journey through life. One should note the signals in life that are the guiding light to perfection. We are part of the puzzle of life.

Life offers signals which guide us to higher understanding of the fabric of life. I choose to respect the signals and follow them to the advantage of all.

# POST SCRIPT

Four years after the CPA (and his wife) passed away:

My phone rings.

I am startled by the flash on my phone

It is the CPA from years ago

How could this be? He has passed away.

It turned out that it was the son who had been in prison.

My heart almost dropped.

We exchanged greetings.

He wanted me to declare that his parents were not in sound mind so he could collect their money.

I declined.

The signs did not fit.

**THE END**

www.ingramcontent.com/pod-product-compliance
Lightning Source LLC
LaVergne TN
LVHW021953060526
838201LV00049B/1695